D0205528

BABY:
An Owner's Manual

BABY:

An Owner's Manual

Operating instructions no Baby should be delivered without

Steve Tague
Julie Long

Broadway Books / New York

PRINTED IN THE UNITED STATES OF AMERICA

BROADWAY BOOKS and its logo, a letter B bisected on the diagonal, are trademarks of Random House, Inc.

Visit our website at www.broadwaybooks.com

First edition published 2003

Concept, book design, and photos by Steve Tague

Library of Congress Cataloging-in-Publication Data

Tague, Steve
    Baby: an owner's manual: operating intructions no baby should be delivered without / Steve Tague, Julie Long.
        p. cm.
        1. Infants—Humor. 2. Infants—Care—Humor. 3. Infants—Care and hygiene—Humor. I. Long, Julie. II. Title.

RJ61.T225 2003
649'.122'0207—dc21   2002043684

ISBN 0-7679-1419-8

10   9   8   7   6   5   4   3   2

Dedications

For my two greatest joys, Dakota and Max, and to the loving memory of their grand-mother, Hisako Tague.

For Brian, who does all things and makes me believe I can, too.

Acknowledgments

The authors wish to thank the following people who made this book possible: Our agent, Tom Connor, for believing in the idea and finding it a home. Patricia Medved at Broadway Books for bringing it to life and nurturing it so skillfully. Beth Datlowe, her assistant, for her hand-holding and humorous e-mails. The sales and marketing department and everyone at Broadway for getting behind the book with such great expectations. Baby Phases of Bend, Mickie Brennan and all of the babies and parents who enabled us to shoot so many wonderful photographs. Dave Caplan of Feedback Graphics, for his skilled hand in helping us meet our dead-line. Barry O'Rourke and Nancy McManus for keeping the creative fire lit under Steve's butt all these years. And our fami-lies and friends who cheered us on, calmed our nerves and fed us material. Special thanks from Steve to Tina Bollman for helping him to find his heart and soul that were missing for so long, and to Julie for sharing a dream and helping make it a reality. Finally, many thanks from Julie to Steve for his great idea and asking her to be part of it.

⚠ WARNING!

WHAT TO DO IF YOU SMELL GAS:
- Do not light match near source.
- Wait 2 minutes.
- If smell persists, remove rear cover carefully to check for leakage.
- If leakage has occurred, discard rear cover along with any debris.
- Clean exhaust area thoroughly and attach new rear cover.

Important Safety Precautions

Read before operating your Baby

When using your Baby, basic safety precautions should always be followed to reduce the risk of damage, personal injury, excessive stress and/or sleepless nights.

Prevent Damage to Unit

- Do not operate your Baby while under the influence of alcohol, drugs or medications.
- Wash hands thoroughly before handling Baby.
- Always hold Baby with both hands and support from underneath.
- Do not obstruct flow of ventilating air.
- Do not let children play on or near Baby.
- Check that cord is unplugged before use.
- Keep exhaust opening and surrounding area free of dirt, dust and accumulated debris.
- Do not place anything heavy on Baby.

M0317A
OBJECT ON BABY WARNING (symbol provided by DBSS)

Important Safety Precautions (cont.)

Read all instructions!

• Do not place Baby on unstable surface.
Unit may fall, resulting in serious damage.

Prevent Injuries

• Always be aware of the risk of injury.

• Keep face at a distance from all moving parts.

• Do not place unit's speakers close to ears.
Baby may emit high-frequency sounds without warning resulting in
serious damage to eardrum.

D1103A
BABY ON TABLE WARNING
(symbol provided by DBSS)

Storage and Placement of Unit

• Never leave Baby near water unattended. Do not submerse completely
in water.

• Place Baby in location with adequate ventilation to prevent heat buildup.

• Do not place Baby in direct sunlight without supervision and sunscreen
protection. Prolonged exposure to sun may cause serious damage to Baby.

• When not in use, store unit in reclined position. Never store unit inverted.

• Avoid extreme heat and cold. Do not place unit in contact with sources of
heat or cold, such as radiators, stoves and freezers.

S0824A
BABY ON RADIATOR WARNING (symbol provided by DBSS)

Miscellaneous Warnings

• To reduce risk of shock, do not expose Baby to electrical outlets, wires
or obnoxious relatives.

• To protect the original finish, do not use any type of abrasive pad or
scouring powder on Baby.

• **To prevent damage or injury to Baby, any repairs and servicing should be
performed by an authorized service provider.**

SAVE THESE INSTRUCTIONS

Introduction

Congratulations on your new Baby! With proper care and handling, your Baby will prove to be the finest investment of your lifetime.

Before you begin operating your Baby, please take a few minutes to read and become familiar with the instructions in this book. On the following pages you will find a wealth of information regarding all aspects of your Baby. By following the instructions carefully, you will be able to fully enjoy and properly maintain your Baby for years to come. Owners are often so satisfied that they order additional units.

NOTE: The instructions appearing in this Owner's Manual are not meant to cover every possible condition and situation that may occur. Common sense and caution must be practiced when operating, maintaining and playing with any Baby.

Table of Contents

Explanation of Symbols

The purpose of the safety symbols is to attract your attention to possible dangers or unpleasant situations. The warning symbols and their explanations deserve your careful attention and understanding. The safety warnings by themselves do not eliminate any danger. The warnings or instructions they give are not substitutes for proper accident prevention measures.

The safety pin is intended to alert the user to important safety instructions that may help avoid damage to unit and/or user.

The bottle indicates a key operating instruction. Failure to follow the instructions as stated can result in less than optimal performance by your Baby.

The water drop indicates a situation in which improper handling could result in the potential for your unit to leak. Leaking can and should be avoided.

The thermometer indicates a situation that may cause your unit to overheat.

The clock indicates an operating procedure of a time-intensive or time-sensitive nature which could impact effective time management.

The safety goggles are intended to alert the user to a situation that could potentially cause eye damage to the owner or to other persons near the Baby.

Features
and Functions

Features and Functions

Available Models

The Baby delivered to you from the factory is a one-of-a-kind, custom creation. Though no two units are exactly alike, your Baby can be classified as one of two base models. Both models function similarly for the first few years and differ primarily in undercarriage design.

fig. 2a

Model BBY-XY-B

 CAUTION: Without rear cover in place, Model BBY-XY-B may spray spontaneously, which can cause burning to eyes. If this occurs, flush eyes with water.

Available Models (cont.)

Identify the model of your unit using the sample photos provided (see figs. 2a and 3a). For future reference, make note of model number under *Product Specifications* (pg. 84), along with height, weight and other information. Some specifications will vary by individual unit.

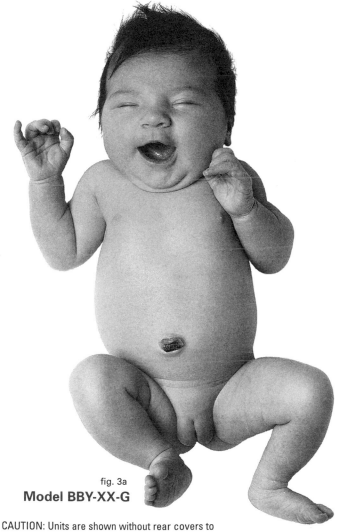

fig. 3a

Model BBY-XX-G

CAUTION: Units are shown without rear covers to provide view of undercarriage. Operating unit without rear cover is not recommended and may result in leaking. See *Changing Rear Cover* (pg. 40).

Features and Functions

Colors and Finishes

The Baby comes in a wide array of colors and finishes, and very few units are identical in appearance.

Exterior Color

The color of your unit's exterior is preset at the factory. Figures 4a–d illustrate just a few of the possible shades. At times your Baby's exterior may appear mottled or two-toned (see fig. 4c). This will cease as unit's circulation system improves over the first 100 hours of operation.

Moonglow   fig. 4a

Peach   fig. 4b

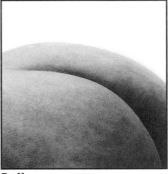

Buff   fig. 4c

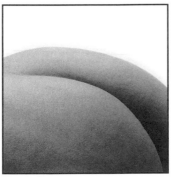

Butt'r Rum   fig. 4d

CAUTION: Always protect unit's finish from direct sunlight. Sunscreen can be used on units six months or older.

Colors and Finishes (cont.)

Lens Color

The manufacturer selects lens color, which may fluctuate before the pigment permanently sets. On units with darker exterior colors, dark lenses will usually not change. On units with lighter exterior color, lens color may change several times during the first six months and up to a year (see figs. 5a–c).

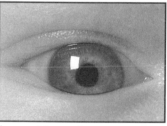

Lens at 1 week.   fig. 5a

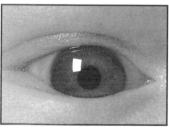

Lens at 2 months.   fig. 5b

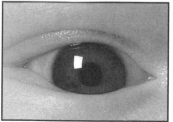

Lens at 6 months.   fig. 5c

Blemishes in the Finish

Your Baby's exterior is made of natural materials and therefore its finish may include slight irregularities. These imperfections only add to the unique character of your individual unit.

Keeping the finish clean and dry will help clear up blemishes. Many blemishes, such as flakes, pimples and rashes disappear within a few days. Others may fade over a period of months or years. Consult your authorized service provider if you have a concern about your unit's finish.

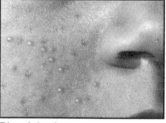

Blemish shown on   fig. 5d
unit's display panel.

CAUTION: Any connecting of dots on unit's exterior should be attempted only with a washable marker.

Features and Functions

Optional Features

In addition to model and color, your new Baby may be customized with other special features.

Convex Cord Socket

When your Baby's factory cord is unplugged after delivery, your unit may possess a convex cord socket instead of a concave socket. This is merely an esthetic variance and will not affect your Baby's performance in any way.

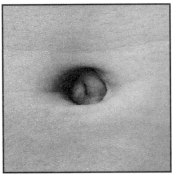

Concave cord socket   fig. 6a

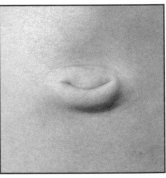

Convex cord socket   fig. 6b

See *Cord Care* (pg. 65) for care and cleaning instructions.

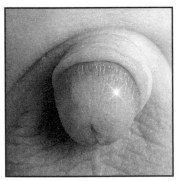

A converted nozzle   fig. 6c
may expose the hidden
beauty of your unit.

Converted Nozzle
Available on Model XY-B only

If you ordered this option on your BABY-XY-B, the original cover on the unit's discharge hose nozzle will be removed. The converted nozzle may have a temporary gauze covering which your authorized service provider may instruct you to change frequently for the first few days. Keep the converted nozzle clean, particularly in the first few days.

ALERT: If redness persists after seven days, consult your authorized service provider.

Optional Features (cont.)

Processor Cover

While all Babies will eventually develop a processor cover, on some units the feature is already in place when delivered. Color, texture and style will vary and may change often over the first year. Units delivered with cover in place may experience a loss of coverage, particularly on the back of the processor (see fig. 7b). This is temporary and will correct itself within a few months.

Some units may have a cover that extends beyond the processor. Refer to *Frequently Asked Questions* (pg. 80).

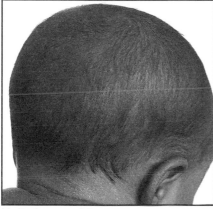

Unit shown with cover.   fig. 7a

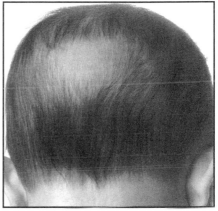

Unit shown with temporary   fig. 7b
loss of coverage.

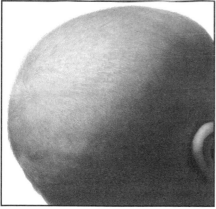

Unit shown with no cover.   fig. 7c

Features and Functions

Diagram of Parts

Your new Baby comes fully equipped with batteries installed. No assembly is necessary. The photo below will help familiarize you with the essential parts of your unit.

NOTE: Parts may shift in transit.

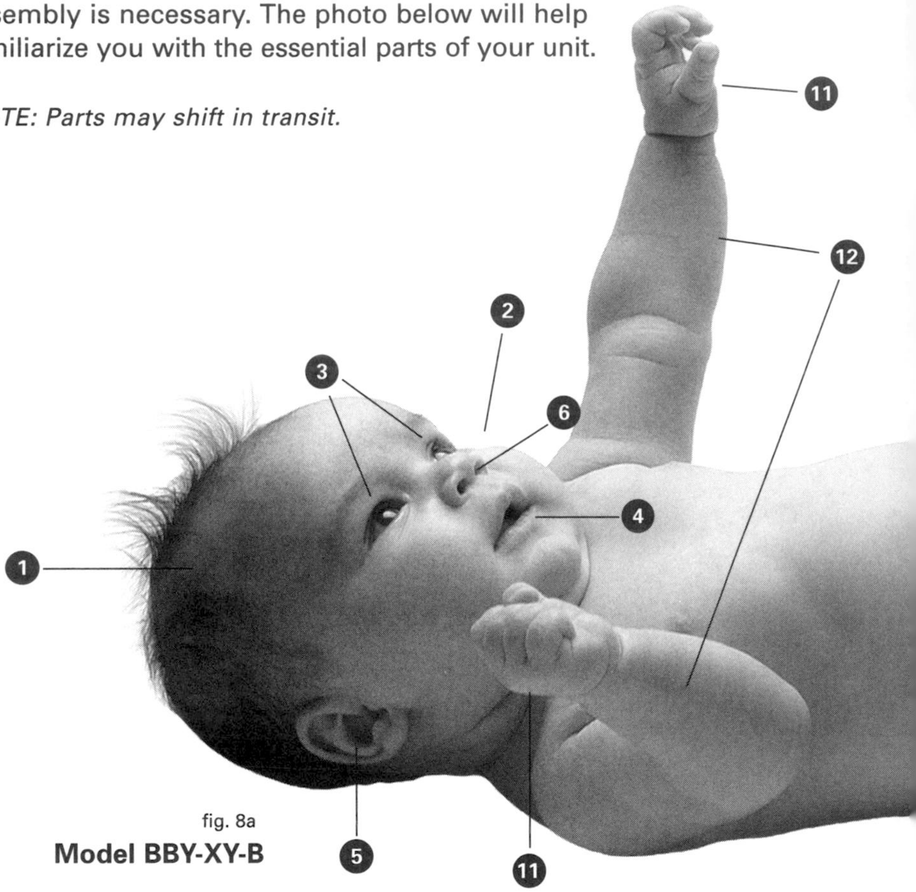

fig. 8a

Model BBY-XY-B

1. **Processor** — Shape may be pointed on delivery but will normalize within two weeks.
2. **Display Panel** — Provides a range of visual and audible signals to operator.
3. **Dual Lenses** — Eight-inch to 14-inch focus power upon delivery.
4. **Intake Valve** — Used to fill unit with fuel. Also functions as overflow valve and speaker.
5. **Audio Sensor** — Highly sensitive especially in sleep mode. Can detect footsteps or whispering from 100 meters.
6. **Smell Sensor** — Also functions as air valve and signals onset of cold.
7. **Cord Socket** — Where factory cord was plugged. Post-production function is as a lint catcher.

Diagram of Parts (cont.)

 WARNING: Keep face and hair away from all moving parts.

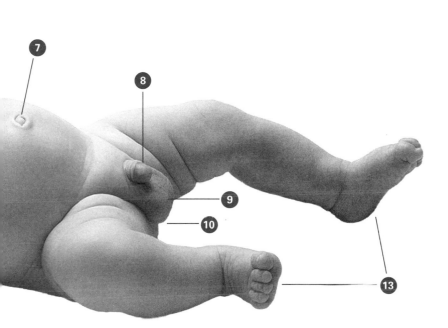

8. **Liquid Discharge Hose** — On model XX-G, a more discreet Discharge Valve serves the same function.
9. **Undercarriage** — If undercarriage on model XY-B appears to be missing, refer to *Unpacking* (pg.17).
10. **Rear Exhaust/Discharge** — Operates automatically as unit's processor signals need.
11. **Grippers** — For grasping. One-ton pulling capacity. Fifth digit may also become intake valve plug.
12. **Extenders** — To increase the reach of Grippers and enable first-stage mobility.
13. **Thrusters** — Enable mobility in various stages, including perambulation by end of first year.

Features and Functions

Main Functions

Your new Baby has four main functions:

Fuel Consumption

The Baby's high-performance engine results in rapid utilization of fuel and the need for frequent refilling. Fuel on demand as unit requires. See *Filling* (pg. 32).

 ALERT: Fill with only high-octane, nonleaded fuel.

Unit refueling.   fig. 10a

Auto-Discharge

Following fuel consumption, discharge will automatically occur. Discharge can take the form of liquids, solids, semi-solids and gas from any of the unit's three emission valves. Though rare, simultaneous discharge from all three valves can occur.

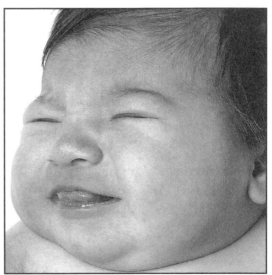

Unit discharging.   fig. 10b

Main Functions (cont.)

Sleep Mode
Your Baby will be in sleep mode for 15 to 18 hours a day. However, these hours will be broken up in units of time too small to allow for rest or productivity of the owner.

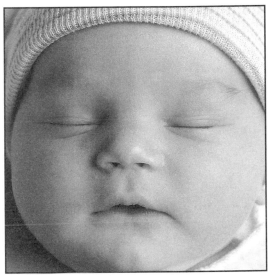

Unit in sleep mode.   fig. 11a

Audio Alert
The Baby's highly sensitive sensor system will detect the need for fuel, rear cover change, sleep or handling. Unit will sound an audible alarm as loud as 10,000 decibels. By process of elimination you can then determine what attention your Baby requires. For units sounding constant audio alert, refer to *Frequently Asked Questions* (pg. 81).

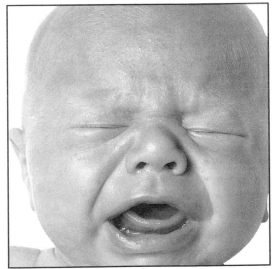

Unit sounding audio alert.   fig. 11b

Features and Functions

Operating Cycle

Typical 12-Hour Cycle of New Unit — A.M. and P.M.

Getting Started

Getting Started

Product Registration

Registration of your Baby is recommended, as it will enable access to value-added services. For example, when a unit is registered with the Social Security Administration it can be claimed as a dependent on your income tax return.

Product registration can be completed immediately upon delivery. When a representative asks you for information to complete your Baby's Certificate of Authenticity, simply state that you would also like an SSN assigned to your unit. A card will be sent to you in the mail as proof of registration.

Should you elect to register your unit at a later date, you will need to complete an application and show evidence of the date and country in which your Baby was delivered. For more information, contact the SSA registration office at 1-800-772-1213 or www.ssa.gov.

It is recommended that you also register your unit with an insurance company to cover regular maintenance and service.

Proof of Registration   fig. 14a
Card with Social
Security Number

NOTE: Store unit's Certificate of Authenticity and Proof of Registration Card in a secure, dry place.

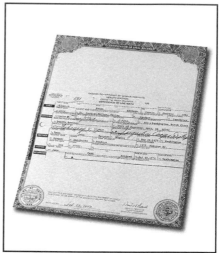

Certificate of Authenticity   fig. 14b

CAUTION: Many Babies look alike. After delivery tag is removed unit may not be easily identifiable. When in possession or vicinity of multiple Babies, consider utilizing a unique covering on your unit(s) to aid in differentiation.

Personalization

You can personalize your Baby by assigning it a code name, which it will learn to recognize over time.

Caution should be used when personalizing to avoid possible ridicule of unit. See the chart below for examples of code names which may produce undesirable effects.

Avoid personalizing as:	If your last name is:
Justin	Case
Candy	Barr
Price	Tague
Miles	Long
Holden	Court
Lance	Boyles
Eileen	Wright
Eaton	Crowe
Ginger	Snapp
Pete	Moss
April	May
Harry	Baer
Doug	Graves
Rose	Bloom
Chris	Crosse
Sonny	Day
Rusty	Bahls

In addition, be aware of the effects of truncation when personalizing your Baby. Owners with last names such as Butt, Horse or Head should avoid the use of code names that can be shortened, such as Harrison, Charles or Richard, respectively.

WARNING: Failure to avoid puns when personalizing can result in damage to unit's exterior as well as internal mechanism.

Getting Started

Unpacking

Unwrapping Unit

To re-create the secure environment in which it was produced, your Baby will be firmly wrapped in a swaddling cloth. This also prevents sudden involuntary jerking of the unit's extenders, which can interrupt sleep mode.

To unwrap your unit, follow the steps shown here. To rewrap unit, simply reverse the steps.

Step 1: Unfold foot flap.

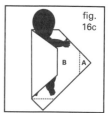

Step 2: Pull side tab A from under unit and open flap B.

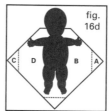

Step 3: Untuck tab C and open flap D.

fig. 16a

Unit secured in protective wrapping.

WARNING: Confinement in older units can interfere with development. To avoid damage to unit, do not store unit tightly wrapped after age of one month.

Unpacking (cont.)

Miscellaneous Packing Materials
Your unit will automatically discharge a black tarry substance known as meconium stool and other internal packing materials in the first few days after delivery.

Removing Delivery Tag
UNDER PENALTY OF LAW THIS TAG NOT TO BE REMOVED EXCEPT BY THE CONSUMER. Before removing delivery tag, check the I.D. to ensure that the unit is the one you ordered. Returns may not be authorized once tag is removed.

To remove delivery tag, insert finger between band and unit and lift. Snip band with scissors, being careful not to cut unit.

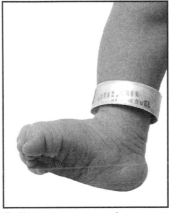

Delivery tag secured   fig. 17a
to unit's thruster.

Inflated Undercarriage
Models XX-G and XY-B
Your unit's undercarriage is inflated for added protection during delivery. This pressure will slowly release as your Baby adjusts to the atmospheric pressure of its environment.

Undescended Undercarriage
Model XY-B only
A small number of XY-B Babies will be shipped with one or both of the undercarriage spheres inside rather than outside the unit. This is not cause for concern. The undercarriage should descend within the first nine months of operation.

WARNING: Do not attempt to manually force undercarriage to descend. Doing so can cause damage to the unit.

Getting Started

Making the Right Connections

The Baby operates via a standard two-way connection. While the primary link is established between the unit and its owner(s), the Baby is wired to accommodate multiple connections.

Care should be taken to ensure that all links are secure. Connect via the following recommended hookups:

* *Handling* (See pg. 28)
* *Filling* (See pg. 32)
* *Changing Rear Cover* (See pg. 40)
* *Maximizing Enjoyment* (See pg. 54)

Unit shown with two-way connection established.   fig. 18a

CAUTION: Loose or improper connections may cause over-heating or distortion in unit.

Items Needed

Your Baby requires just a few essential items for proper functioning and safe operation. In addition, accessories are available to enhance efficiency and enjoyment for both you and your Baby.

For optimal results, review the following pages and stock necessary items before delivery of your unit.

Getting Started

Items Needed (cont.)

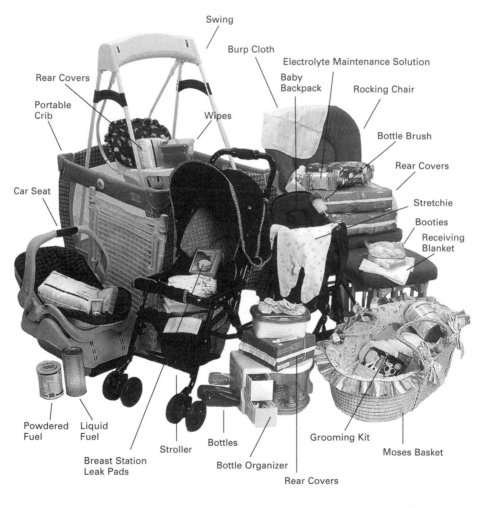

Swing

Burp Cloth

Electrolyte Maintenance Solution

Rear Covers

Baby Backpack

Rocking Chair

Portable Crib

Wipes

Bottle Brush

Rear Covers

Car Seat

Stretchie

Booties

Receiving Blanket

Powdered Fuel

Liquid Fuel

Stroller

Bottles

Grooming Kit

Moses Basket

Breast Station Leak Pads

Bottle Organizer

Rear Covers

fig. 20a

Note: For help acquiring necessary items, consider a predelivery party. Truck rental is recommended to assist in transporting the equipment to Baby's home base location.

Items Needed (cont.)

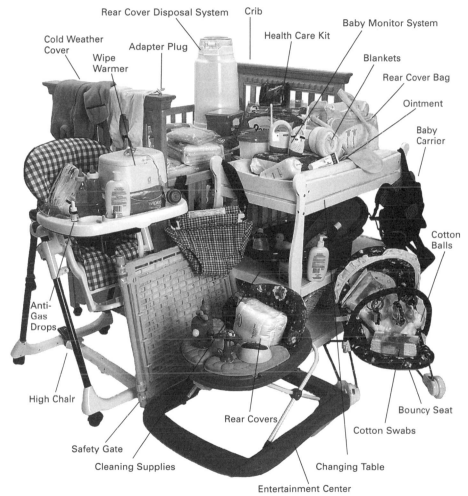

Rear Cover Disposal System Crib

Baby Monitor System

Cold Weather Cover

Adapter Plug

Health Care Kit

Wipe Warmer

Blankets

Rear Cover Bag

Ointment

Baby Carrier

Cotton Balls

Anti-Gas Drops

High Chair

Bouncy Seat

Rear Covers

Cotton Swabs

Safety Gate

Changing Table

Cleaning Supplies

Entertainment Center

fig. 21a

Getting Started

Items Needed (cont.)

The following is a checklist of recommended items, grouped by unit's primary functions:

For Filling
Via Breast Station
- Drop cloth
- Breast pump (optional)

Via Bottle Terminal
- Bottles (4 oz. and 8 oz.)
- Nipple units
- Disposable liners (optional)
- Fuel formula (liquid or concentrate)
- Bottle brush
- Measuring cup
- Spoon
- Sterilization container
- Tongs

Via Solid Fuel
- Filling station (seated style)
- Protective covering for Baby and owner
- Prepackaged fuel
- Spoon
- Cleaning wipes

For Covering
- Rear covers (12 dozen to start)
- Undergarments
- Rompers
- Stretchies
- Drawstring sacks
- Sleepwear
- Sweater
- Hat
- Booties/socks
- Bibs
- Bunting

For Cleaning and Maintenance
- Containment site for hazardous materials
- Cleanser wipes
- Baby soap
- Baby shampoo
- Cotton swabs
- Ointment
- Baby powder or corn starch
- Rubbing alcohol
- Petroleum jelly
- Saline drops
- Aspirator
- Nail scissors
- Brush and comb

CAUTION: Store unit in location with adequate ventilation to prevent heat buildup.

For Storing
- Adapter plug for unit's intake valve
- Remote monitoring device
- Cradle
- Crib with mattress and bumper
- Receiving blankets for swaddling

For Transporting
- Large moving van
- Car seat
- Stroller
- Snuggly or other carrier
- Travel bag (consider model with wheels)

For Owner Sanity
- Winning lottery ticket
- Earplugs
- Remote control (see pg. 56)
- Caffeine
- Anti-gas drops

WARNING: Though at times tempting, do not operate Baby under the influence of alcohol, drugs or heavy medication.

Items Needed (cont.)

Your Baby as an Accessory
Your Baby is designed to complement any style of dress.

Formal Attire   fig. 23a

Casual Dress   fig. 23b

Sporting Apparel   fig. 23c

WARNING: Use only Baby carrying devices. Do not carry Baby in purse or shoulder bag, or attach to owner with duct tape and/or rope.

Getting Started

Setting Baby's Clock

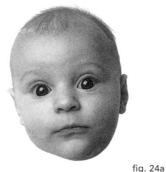

fig. 24a

12:15 PM – CORRECT

fig. 24b

12:15 PM – INCORRECT

fig. 24c

12:15 AM – CORRECT

fig. 24d

12:15 AM – INCORRECT

WARNING: Once set, Baby's internal clock may be permanent. Do not confuse A.M. and P.M.

Setting Baby's Clock (cont.)

Accurate setting of unit's internal clock is crucial for proper scheduling of daily functions. Failure to set clock correctly can result in sleeplessness in owner.

To set Baby's clock, undertake the cleaning, filling and storing functions at approximately the same time every day. When filling at night, keep lights and TV off to avoid stimulating unit. Infomercials and B movies can seriously hamper ability to set unit's clock.

Setting unit's clock may take from six to 12 weeks or longer.

 CAUTION: Failure to follow a schedule for Baby's functions may cause unit to overheat.

Language Selection

The Baby comes wired to accept a limitless variety of language programs. Once you select a language preference, maintain consistency. Do not switch languages.

Unit may be programmed using the bilingual option. If electing to utilize bilingual language programming, one primary or other significant connection should communicate with unit exclusively in the second language.

Regardless of which language(s) you select, it will take more than a year for your Baby's processor to be programmed. Until this time, your Baby will utilize its factory-set language.

 CAUTION: Do not adopt Baby's factory-set language, as this will limit the unit's ability to communicate with others and may result in ridicule toward Baby and/or owner.

Basic Operation

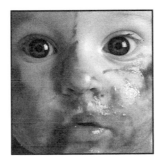

Basic Operation

Handling

Lifting Unit—Display Panel Up

Step 1: Support rear and processor fig. 28a

Step 2: Lift fig. 28b

Step 3: Cradle fig. 28c

HANDLE WITH CARE: Babies under eight weeks of age have weak structural systems. To avoid damage to unit, always support Baby's processor.

Handling (cont.)

Lifting Unit—Display Panel Down

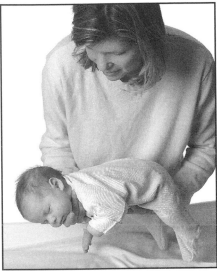

NOTE: Handling unit can feel awkward in the beginning. Though the new unit is fragile and should not be dropped, do not be afraid to pick it up.

WARNING: Although it can cause dry skin on operator, hands must be washed before picking up Baby.

Step 1: Support midsection and processor   fig. 29a

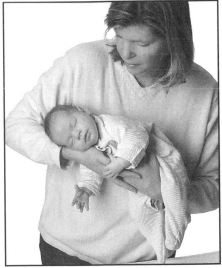

Step 2: Lift and twist   fig. 29b

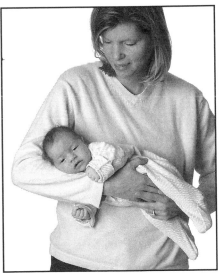

Step 3: Cradle   fig. 29c

29

Basic Operation

Handling

Holding Unit Correctly

The Cradle   fig. 30a

The Inverted Cradle   fig. 30b

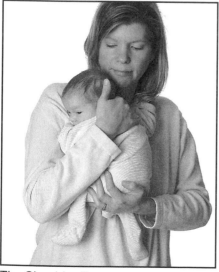

The Shoulder Rest   fig. 30c

Handling (cont.)

Holding Unit Incorrectly

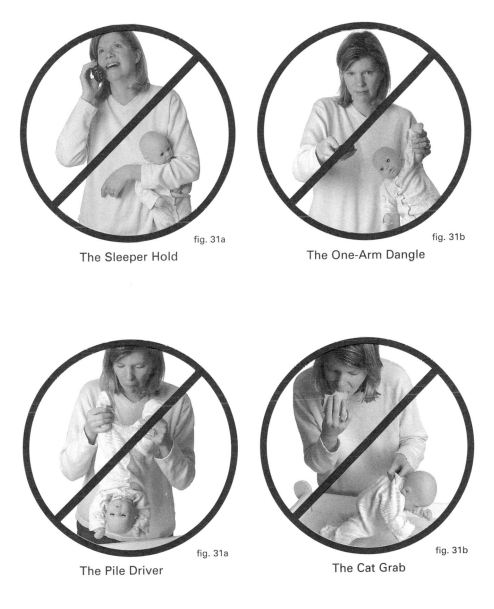

fig. 31a
The Sleeper Hold

fig. 31b
The One-Arm Dangle

fig. 31a
The Pile Driver

fig. 31b
The Cat Grab

Basic Operation

Filling

Your Baby's fuel tank should be filled on demand, as indicated by unit's audio alert system. With new models, refilling may be needed every two hours or continuously at times.

Fueling can be handled at the breast station or bottle terminal, or a combination of both. To determine your preferred method, review the pros and cons below.

Breast Station Pros and Cons

Pros

- Fuel formulated to help prevent contaminants from infecting Baby
- Low cost
- No preparation, highly portable
- Burns extra calories/day in owner, aiding post-delivery weight loss
- Aids in making strong connections

Cons

- More time-intensive
- Imprecise fuel consumption measurement
- Cannot substitute fueling attendants, which can result in sleep deprivation and resentment
- Possible leakage and/or disproportion of breast station
- Fueling formulation dependent on attendant's fuel intake
- Former sex toy becomes primarily utilitarian

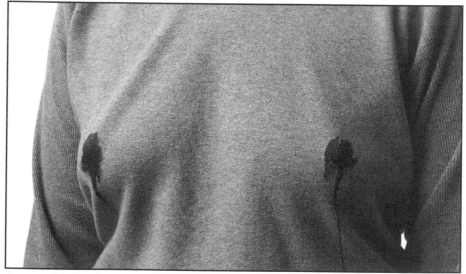

A potential disadvantage of filling via breast station is nozzle leakage.   fig. 32a

Filling (cont.)

Bottle Terminal Pros and Cons

Pros

- Precise fuel consumption measurement
- Can utilize team of fueling attendants
- Greater flexibility in owner's schedule
- Consistent formulation
- Baby requires less frequent fillings
- Doesn't stir controversy for fueling in public places

Cons

- No protection against infection by contaminants
- Costly
- Requires additional equipment (sold separately)
- Requires preparation time
- Need to clean and sterilize bottle terminals

Filling via bottle station requires purchasing and maintaining additional equipment.

fig. 33a

33

Basic Operation

Filling (cont.)

Filling at Breast Station

Filling at the Breast Station takes practice. Not all units latch on immediately. If problem persists, contact your authorized service provider for assistance or a referral to a breast-filling specialist.

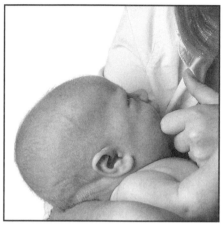

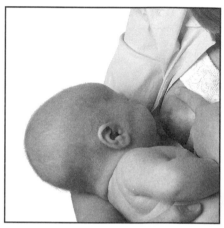

Step 1: With unit in cradle hold, trigger rooting reflex by stroking unit near intake valve. fig. 34a

Step 2: Guide entire nozzle into unit's intake valve. fig. 34b

Step 3: Check that unit is securely latched and a tight seal has formed. Fill unit until breast station is drained. fig. 34c

Step 4: Break suction by inserting little finger into side of unit's intake valve. Remove Baby and release excess gas (see pg. 37). fig. 34d

Filling (cont.)

Step 5: Transfer Baby to other breast station to ensure adequate fuel supply and to extend the life of filling nozzles. Repeat steps 1–4 and release excess gas again.

NOTE: For remote filling, see Frequently Asked Questions *(pg. 81).*

 FILLING CAN BE TIME-CONSUMING. For scheduling purposes, double the original estimated time for fueling.

fig. 35a

Failure to alternate breast stations can alter size uniformity.

fig. 35b

Unilateral feeding may help to offset a preexisting lopsided condition.

 WARNING: Cracking and bleeding may occur at nozzles. Keep ice packs or frozen peas on hand, and expose nozzles to air whenever possible.

 CAUTION: After the first four months of operation, unit may begin teething. Filling unit at breast station during this time period may cause discomfort.

35

Basic Operation

Filling (cont.)

Filling at Bottle Terminal (Equipment and fuel sold separately)
Before you begin: Wash and rinse all bottles (unless using disposable liners), nipples, rings, discs and caps. Sterilize in boiling water (for 10 minutes), in sterilizer, or in dishwasher with water temperature of at least 180°F (82°C).

Prepare fuel formula according to manufacturer's instructions. To minimize waste, begin with small bottles until your unit's fuel capacity has been determined. For added convenience, fill a number of bottles at one time and keep refrigerated.

Step 1.
Warm fuel by placing bottle in bowl of hot water for several minutes. Fuel can also be given cold, if unit will accept it.

Step 2.
Check fuel temperature by shaking a few drops onto your wrist. Fuel should be at room temperature or warm, never hot.

Step 3.
With unit in cradle hold, trigger rooting reflex by stroking unit near intake valve. Insert bottle nipple into unit's intake valve.

Step 4.
Hold bottle at a 45-degree angle. Increase angle as needed to maintain air-free flow of fuel.

Step 5.
To remove bottle, break suction by inserting little finger into side of unit's intake valve. Release excess gas (see pg. 37).

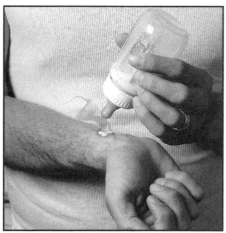

If welt forms on wrist, fuel is too hot. Cool and test again.   fig. 36a

WARNING: Never warm fuel in microwave. Uneven heating can cause burns.

36 BABY: An Owner's Manual

Releasing Excess Gas

During filling at breast station or bottle terminal, your Baby will intake air in addition to fuel. This buildup of excess gas creates undue pressure on the unit and should be released intermittently throughout the filling process. Failure to manually release gas may cause displacement of gas through rear exhaust and/or extreme discomfort in unit as indicated by audio alert.

Gas Release Methods

Rear-Facing Release
Position unit against your shoulder while supporting rear cover. Pat or rub back of unit until pressure releases via intake valve.

Prone Release
Lie unit facedown on lap surface and hold securely. Pat or rub back of unit until pressure releases via intake valve.

Upright Release
Sit unit on lap surface with unit's top supported and leaning slightly forward. Pat or rub back of unit until pressure releases via intake valve.

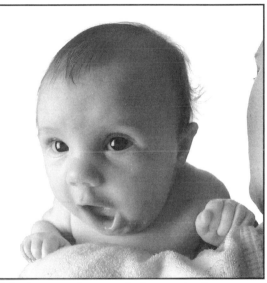

Unit shown using rear-facing method to release excess gas.   fig. 37b

fig. 37a

Maintain safe distance from unit's intake valve immediately after filling and prior to releasing excess gas.

WARNING: Manual gas release may be accompanied by a degree of fuel spillage. Protect fabrics to prevent staining. Wipe up any spilled fuel immediately.

CAUTION: Failure to release excess gas may cause the unit's intake function to stall. This should not be mistaken as an indication that the fuel tank is full. Release excess gas and continue the filling process.

37

Basic Operation

Advanced Filling

When your Baby is between four and six months, the unit will require the added power of solid fuel. For optimum performance, fill unit with a blend of solid and liquid fuels. Failure to maintain proper fuel mixture ratio may result in fuel-line blockage and/or malfunction of rear exhaust.

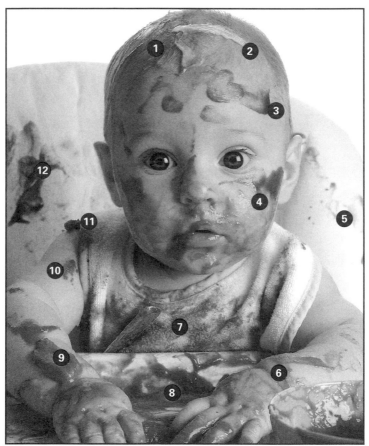

fig. 38a

Model B shown utilizing variety of solid fuels. Shown here:

1. Peas	5. Carrots	9. Creamed Spinach
2. Bananas	6. Yams	10. Oatmeal w/ fruit
3. Prunes	7. Green Beans	11. Rice Cereal w/ fruit
4. Apricot	8. Peaches	12. Apple Blueberry

Advanced Filling (cont.)

10 Steps to Effective Filling

1. **Protect** unit and surrounding area from fuel spillage.

2. **Secure** unit in a filling station according to manufacturer's instructions.

3. **Select** a fuel. Rice cereal is recommended as first solid fuel.

4. **Introduce** fuel to unit by placing a small amount on filling station tray. Allow unit to interact with fuel (see fig. 38a).

5. **Spoon** a small amount of fuel into unit's intake valve. Spillage of fuel out of valve is common as unit's motor functions adjust to new input.

6. **Wait** for response as unit's taste sensors process input. If fuel is accepted, intake valve will reopen; proceed to Step 7. If unit rejects fuel, repeat Steps 4 and 5 once more. If fuel is still rejected, proceed to Step 9.

7. **Repeat** Step 5 at frequent intervals.

8. **Stop Filling** when unit signals full tank (e.g., audio alarm, sealed intake valve, fuel projected or propelled).

9. **Clean** unit and surrounding area thoroughly. Store unused fuel in refrigerator in tightly sealed container.

10. **Supplement** solid fuel with liquid fuel from breast station or bottle terminal.

Mixing Fuels

Your Baby can utilize many different solid fuels. Introduce new fuels individually. Wait 2–3 days after each fuel addition to rule out any negative reaction.

Self-filling

As unit's functionality advances, it will begin to fill itself. Self-filling may occur with or without a utensil. Serve fuel only on shatterproof plastic materials. Always supervise self-filling.

CAUTION: DO NOT OVERFILL.
Overfilling or topping off tank can result in projectile discharge of fuel without warning.

CAUTION: Self-filling is a time-consuming function. Allow sufficient time for both fueling and post-fueling cleanup.

Basic Operation

Changing Rear Cover

Your Baby's auto-discharge will function up to 20 times per day. A rear cover change is required after each emission.

To change rear cover, follow the steps shown on pages 41–43. Early changes may take up to 15 minutes, at which time you may need to change unit again.

NOTE: Rear covers are sold separately and are available in disposable or reusable varieties. Selection is at the discretion of the operator.

WARNING: Failure to change rear cover after each discharge can result in discoloration and/or corrosion on unit's exterior surface.

WARNING: Discharge quantities vary and may be large at times. Emissions may leak from rear cover, particularly semisolid discharges from rear exhaust, and may contaminate all surrounding surfaces. Be prepared to sterilize all surfaces following rear cover change.

Changing Rear Cover (cont.)
Step 1: Sniff Test

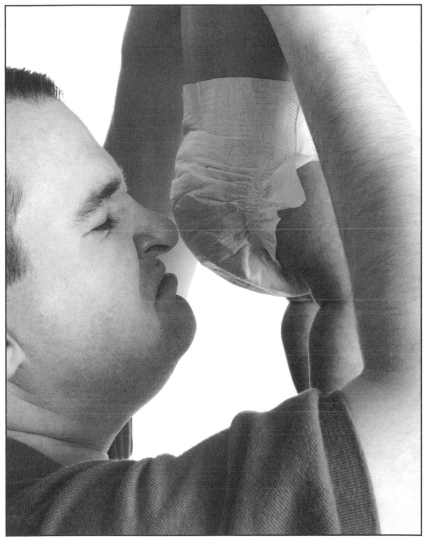

If ammonia or other strong odor is detected, prepare to change rear cover. *NOTE: With new units, noisy emissions may make the sniff test unnecessary.*

fig. 41a

Basic Operation

Changing Rear Cover (cont.)

NOTE: Use of gas mask and gloves are optional. Self-cleaning units are not available.

Step 2: Detach Cover.

Unfasten sides of cover and lower front flap.   fig. 42a

Step 3: Remove Debris.

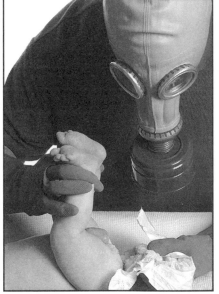

Grasp thrusters and lift unit.   fig. 42b
Use front flap of cover to clear any debris. Remove soiled cover and discard in waste bag or container.

CAUTION: Fresh air can stimulate spontaneous spraying in Model XY-B. Lower front flap slowly.

Changing Rear Cover (cont.)

Step 4: Sanitize.

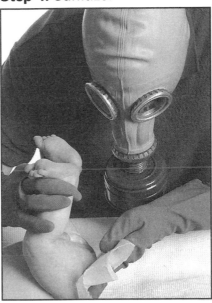

fig. 43a

Clean unit's undercarriage
and rear exhaust area (see
pg. 64). Allow surface to air
dry, then lubricate (see pg. 68).

Step 5: Attach New Cover.

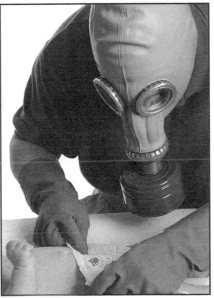

fig. 43b

Slide new cover under unit
and lower thrusters. Fold
front flap up to meet back
flap and fasten at sides.

 ALERT: To minimize the potential for
leakage, choose a rear cover size that
fits snuggly on unit.

Basic Operation

Attaching Body Covers

Your Baby's finish can be protected from daily wear and tear, as well as environmental elements, by utilizing body covers. Body covers are sold separately and are available in a wide variety of styles and colors. Figs. 45a–d illustrate proper covering technique for one of the most popular models, the full jumpsuit.

Incorrectly Attached

fig. 44a

Unit shown incorrectly covered in jumpsuit.

Attaching Body Covers (cont.)
How to Correctly Attach Cover

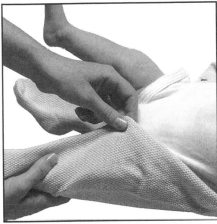

Step 1: Lay unit on open jumpsuit. Insert right thruster into cover slot A, and left thruster B into cover slot B.　fig. 45a

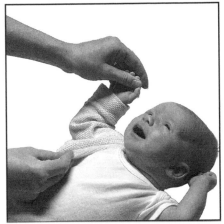

Step 2: Insert right gripper into cover slot C and left gripper into cover slot D.　fig. 45b

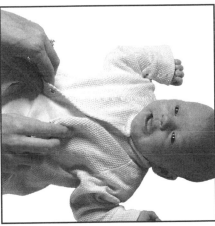

Step 3: Pull right and left cover flaps together and snap into place, making certain snaps are properly aligned.　fig. 45c

Unit shown correctly covered in jumpsuit.　fig. 45d

Basic Operation

Storing

Store your Baby in a clean, dry place at room temperature and away from direct sources of heat. Use only certified Baby storage containers that meet Consumer Products Safety Codes. Place containers on a hard, level surface and store unit with display panel up. When storing unit in a remote location, consider using a monitor.

Storage for Sleep Mode
Store new units in a portable container for convenience (see fig. 46a). Older units should be stored in a crib (see fig. 46b).

Moses Basket   fig. 46a

Crib (Unit shown with optional   fig. 46b
adapter plug to aid transition
from filling to storing.)

 WARNING: Do not store unit on appliances such as a dryer or stove.

Storing (cont.)

Other Storage Options

Baby can be secured in a reclined seat for interaction with owner and/or environment (see fig. 47a).

When storing on the ground, lay unit on a protective covering (see fig. 47b).

Baby Seat   fig. 47a

Ground storage using optional   fig. 47b
Baby gym.

Swing   fig. 47c

Swing storage will often lull unit into sleep mode. While this convenience may be attractive, unit should not be stored in swing permanently (see fig 47c).

NOTE: For mobile storage options, see Transporting *(pg. 52).*

WARNING: If using battery-operated swing, keep backup batteries on hand at all times to avoid unit overheating.

47

Basic Operation

Reading Display Panel

Your Baby's display panel will indicate the unit's operational status and/or signal when unit requires attention (see fig. 48a and figs. 49a–f).

fig. 48a

Unit running smoothly.

Reading Display Panel (cont.)

Unit requires refilling. fig. 49a

Unit overheating. fig. 49b

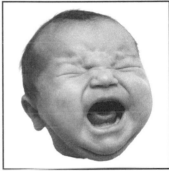

Unit requires handling. fig. 49c

Unit should be stored. fig. 49d

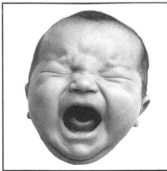

Unit's rear cover fig. 49e
should be changed.

Unit self-testing fig. 49f
audio alert system.

49

Advanced Operation

Advanced Operation

Transporting

Your Baby is fully portable, enabling you to enjoy ownership on the go. (Modes of transportation sold separately.)

Car Seat

Car seats are required by law for automotive transport. Follow manufacturer's instructions and face units under 21 lb. (9 kg) toward the rear of the vehicle.

 WARNING: Never transport Baby without substantial supply of fuel and rear covers.

Car seats can also be used as Baby carriers.   fig. 52a

Stroller

If you are traveling on foot, a stroller can be useful.

Carrier

A Baby carrier provides hands-free transportation (see fig. 53a on next page). For other carrier options, refer to *Your Baby as an Accessory* (pg. 23).

 ALERT: Preparing to transport unit can be time-consuming. To avoid a delayed departure, double your allotted prep time.

Strollers can double as shopping carts.   fig. 52b

Transporting (cont.)

Air Travel

Gathering and transporting the required accessories for air travel may be time-consuming and difficult. Allow plenty of time. When transporting unit on airplane, prevent air pressure buildup by filling unit or inserting adapter plug during takeoff and landing.

Unit shown in hands-free carrier with necessary supplies in tow.

fig. 53a

 WARNING: When traveling by plane, never stow Baby in overhead compartment or underneath the seat in front of you.

Advanced Operation

Maximizing Enjoyment

Your Baby is wired for stimulus/response interchange, which should be a regular part of its daily operation. While interactive operation can grow in complexity over time, don't expect a new unit to respond to advanced play such as golf, poker or violin.

Some games that your new Baby will immediately respond to include:
- Airplane
- Bouncing on Knee
- Peek-a-Boo
- Pat-a-Cake
- This Little Piggy
- Sooo Big

 CAUTION: Avoid inverted play (such as Airplane) immediately after filling unit.

To avoid negative response, always test your Peek-a-Boo face in a mirror before using on unit and carefully screen the faces of substitute players.

fig. 54a

Maximizing Enjoyment (cont.)

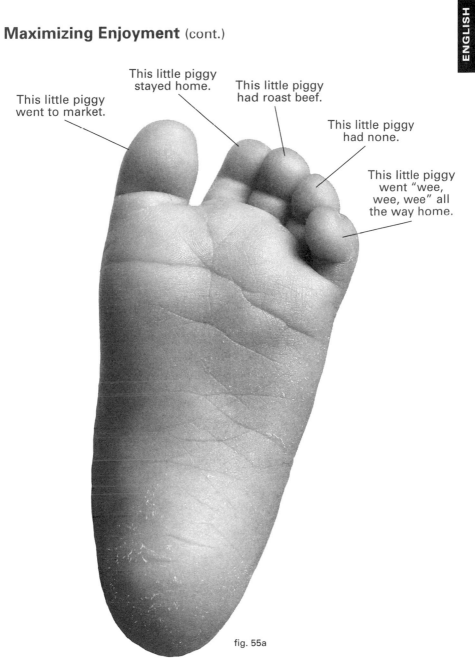

This little piggy went to market.

This little piggy stayed home.

This little piggy had roast beef.

This little piggy had none.

This little piggy went "wee, wee, wee" all the way home.

fig. 55a

Proper recitation and toe assignment for "This Little Piggy."

Advanced Operation

Remote Control

The remote control convenience can minimize exertion and enable you to recharge your own power supply.

Remotes are available in several different styles:

- Spousal Remote
- Relative Remote
- Universal Remote

Universal remotes can be found in the Yellow Pages under "Nanny." Select this and other remotes with care.

Activating Remote

To activate the remote, always preface command with words like "honey" or "I'm exhausted." Programmed correctly, your remote can perform complex functions.

Parental Control

This feature prevents your Baby from being exposed to certain stimuli, including remotes, that may be unnecessary or unwanted. Exercise parental control to restrict language and any undesirable commands that might be used on your Baby.

 CAUTION: Remotes provide limited power supply and will drain quickly. Replace frequently.

Remote Control (cont.)

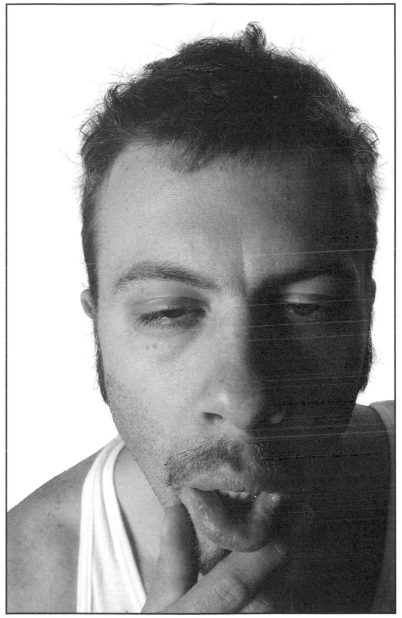

Spousal remote shown with low battery power.

fig. 57a

Advanced Operation

Operating in Extreme Temperatures

Body Cover for Cold Weather

Add an additional layer of covering for warmth. In near-freezing temperatures, cover unit's processor, audio sensors, grippers and thrusters. In very cold or windy weather, wrap a scarf around unit's display panel.

fig. 58a
Model XY-B shown in 1-piece winter cover with optional hood ornaments.

WARNING: Do not block unit's smell sensor/air valve.

Operating in Extreme Temperatures (cont.)

Body Cover for Hot Weather

Keep Baby from overheating by minimizing body covers and avoiding exposure to direct sunlight. Protect unit's finish by storing in the shade and coating finish with sunscreen. Use appropriate covers on processor and lenses.

fig. 59a
Model XX-G shown
in 2 piece beach attire
(top piece optional).

NOTE: Any similarity between Baby and any rock star is purely coincidental and unintentional.

ALERT: On units under 6 months, consult your authorized service provider before applying sunscreen.

59

Advanced Operation

Fine-Tuning Sound System

For your listening pleasure you may wish to fine-tune the Baby's state-of-the-art sound system.

Volume Control
There is no volume control on the Baby. However, the installation of sound-absorbing material in Baby's room may reduce excessive noise levels. Heavy curtains and soft furnishings provide sound absorption and add less reverberate quality to the upper octaves of the Baby's audio range.

Mute Button
To temporarily mute Baby's audio output, insert an adapter plug into unit's intake valve (see fig. 60a).

Unit shown with audio muted via adapter plug.   fig. 60a

 CAUTION: Use of adapter plug beyond six months may cause plug to become permanent.

Stereo Sound
This option can be achieved with the addition of a second Baby (see fig. 60b) or the use of an electronic Baby monitor to simulate stereo sound.

NOTE: You may receive the stereo sound feature even when it was not ordered.

Stereo sound in effect.   fig. 60b

Fine-Tuning Sound System (cont.)

Surround Sound

By adding several Babies you can create the feeling of reflective sound that surrounds you in a movie theater or concert hall. This option requires the strategic placement of Babies around the room (see fig. 61a). To sample surround sound, visit your local day-care establishment.

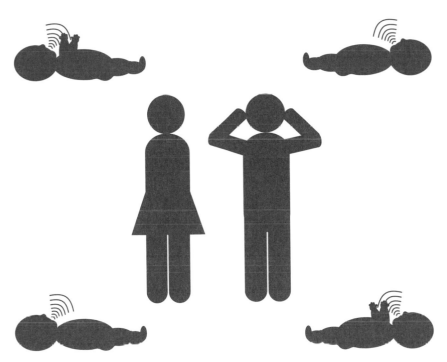

Proper placement of Babies in room for surround sound effect.   fig. 61a

WARNING: Close proximity to unit's speakers when at full volume can cause hearing loss. Maintain a safe distance or wear protective earplugs.

Cleaning and Maintenance

Cleaning and Maintenance

Spot Cleaning

Spot clean the exposed areas of your Baby daily, and the undercarriage each time the rear cover is changed. Use warm tap water with cotton balls or clean wash cloth. Gently wipe all folds and creases. Use a separate cotton ball or clean section of the cloth for each pass. Pat dry with a clean towel as you finish each section.

NOTE: After spot cleaning, lubrication is recommended to maintain unit's finish. See pg. 68.

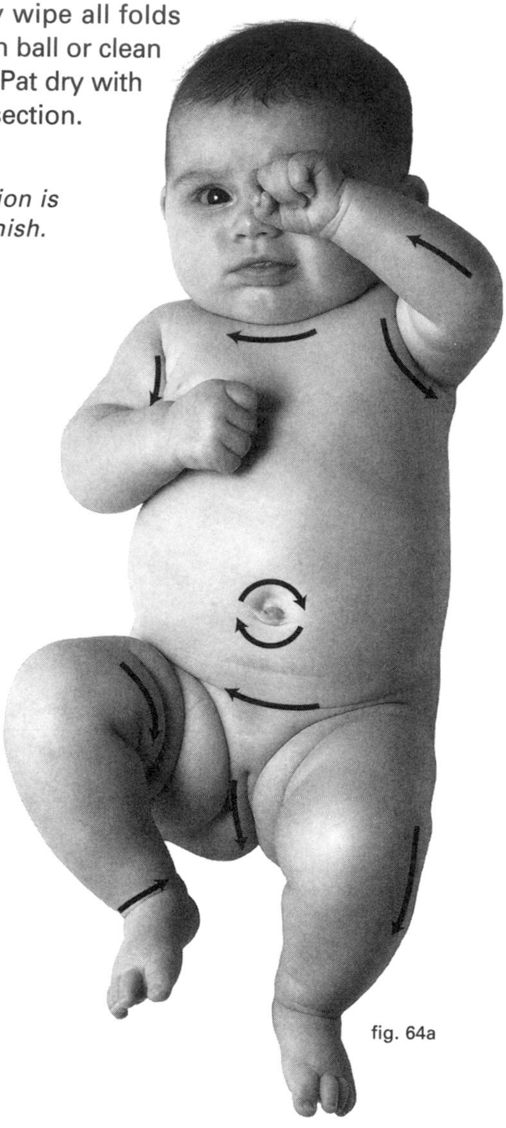

fig. 64a

ALERT: Do not use scouring powders or solvents on Baby, as they can scratch and/or dull the finish.

Wipe Baby in directions indicated by the arrows.

Spot Cleaning (cont.)

Cord Care

When your unit is delivered and unplugged, it will take approximately 10 days for the end of the factory cord to disengage from the Baby's cord socket. During this transition, it is important to keep the area clean and dry. Expose to air as much as possible. Clean the cord daily with alcohol to avoid infection and hasten the drying process. Once cord has disengaged, continue to clean the cord socket daily until it is fully healed.

Converted Nozzle Care
Model XY-B only

If you selected the converted nozzle option (pg. 6) on your Baby, keep the area as clean and dry as possible for the first few days. Wipe nozzle gently with soap and water whenever rear cover is changed. Your delivery representative may also direct you to cover nozzle with fresh gauze and petroleum jelly. Avoid submerging nozzle in water.

The tip of the nozzle may appear red and/or secrete a yellow substance. Both are normal occurrences and should dissipate within a week. If redness and secretion continue past this time period, consult your authorized service provider.

Cleaning Inside of Unit

The inside of your Baby is self-cleaning and needs no special care. DO NOT ATTEMPT TO CLEAN INSIDE THE AUDIO SENSORS, SMELL SENSOR, REAR EXHAUST OR INTAKE VALVE. Any discharge around openings can be gently wiped with a cotton ball or cloth. If unit's smell sensor is clogged, suction sensor with an aspirator.

 ALERT: If discharge occurs from cord or cord socket, contact your authorized service provider.

Cleaning and Maintenance

Washing Unit

NOTE: Until unit's factory cord is disengaged and fully healed, utilize spot cleaning in place of washing (see pg. 64).

Periodically clean Baby with soap and water. Hand wash with a non-abrasive mild Baby cleanser. Do not wash in dishwasher, including top rack. Wash in kitchen sink or small basin. Water should be warm but not hot. Do not exceed 85°F (30°C).

Do not immerse unit's display panel and audio sensors. Wipe these areas with moistened cotton ball prior to inserting unit into wash tub.

After washing and rinsing, remove unit from tub and pat dry with clean towel. Ensure all creases and folds are thoroughly dry, then lubricate (see pp. 68–69).

Hold Baby securely when washing, as it can be slippery when wet.   fig. 66a

Washing Unit (cont.)

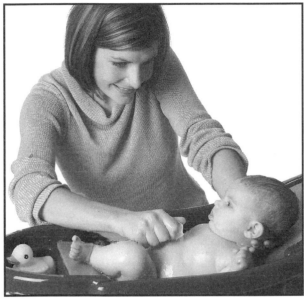

Support unit at all times and never
leave Baby unattended. *NOTE: Check for
gas leaks while rear exhaust is submerged.*

fig. 67a

Washing Processor Cover
Wash with mild shampoo, work-
ing gently over soft spots and
avoiding unit's lenses and display
panel. Rinse well. Towel dry. Style
as desired.

fig. 67b

CAUTION: Washing processor cover
may induce Baby's audio alert and
cause unit to temporarily overheat.
Work quickly.

Do not use standard household
cleaning utensils on Baby. See
Items Needed (pg. 22).

Cleaning and Maintenance

Lubrication Chart

Lubrication is recommended after cleaning Baby, and during certain maintenance functions. The charts below identify the locations requiring lubrication and what lubricant to utilize.

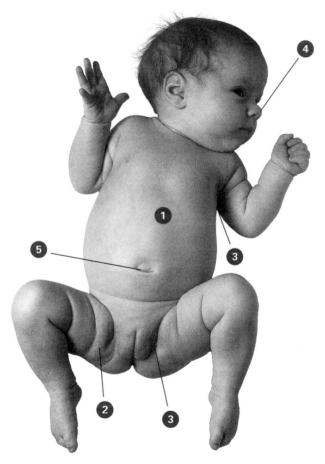

Model XX-G shown.   fig. 68a

1. **Oil** — Apply liberally to Baby's finish to maintain original softness.
2. **Ointment** — Spread a thin film on undercarriage and around rear exhaust as a barrier to liquid discharge, to prevent and heal corrosion.
3. **Powder** — Dust in folds and crevices to reduce friction between moving parts.

Lubrication Chart (cont.)

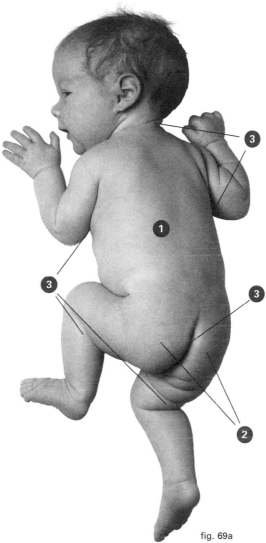

fig. 69a

4. **Saline** — Apply with an aspirator to loosen and remove blockage in smell sensor.

5. **Alcohol** — Use with cotton ball to clean during transitioning from cord to socket.

Cleaning and Maintenance

Trimming

Trim excessive growth on tips of Baby's grippers and thrusters. Use blunt-ended Baby scissors (sold separately) for best results. Cut gripper tips following the natural curve. Cut thruster tips straight across. Do not cut surface of grippers or thrusters.

 WARNING: Do not attempt to trim using household shears or other tools.

Protective gloves are an alternative to trimming new unit.   fig. 70a

 WARNING: Failure to trim tips of grippers can result in a scratched finish or damage to owner, especially on face.

Cleaning and Maintenance

Corrosion

Exposure to excess moisture for prolonged periods of time can corrode the surface of Baby's undercarriage and rear exhaust areas.

Preventive and maintenance measures include:

• Change rear cover frequently
• Thoroughly clean and dry surface
• Keep rear cover removed to expose area to air
• Apply protectant
• Avoid plastic outer covers

Deposit Buildup
In some units, flaky deposits can build up on unit's processor. To remove, apply a thin layer of oil to surface. Leave overnight, then brush or wash processor. Repeat as needed.

ALERT: If corrosion or deposits remain or spread, contact an authorized service provider.

Cleaning and Maintenance

Scheduled Maintenance

The Baby is a precision-engineered machine and requires service at regular intervals to keep it running smoothly. Use only authorized service providers (see pg. 83).

Mileage may vary from unit to unit. Intervals indicate months or miles, whichever comes first.

Service Required	1 mo. or 1,000 miles	2 mos. or 2,000 miles
Check:		
Body		
Soft spots	■	■
Lens auto-focus	■	■
Audio sensors	■	■
Intake valve	■	■
Motor	■	■
Air filters	■	■
Thrusters	■	■
Grippers	■	■
Undercarriage	■	■
Measure:		
Length	■	■
Weight	■	■
Processor circumference	■	■
Additives:		
Hepatitis B		■
DTaP*		■
HIB**		■
Polio		■
MMR***		

*Diptheria, Tetanus and Pertussis
**H. Influenza Type B
***Measles, Mumps, Rubella

Scheduled Maintenance (cont.)

The intervals indicated are based on Baby operating under normal conditions. Additional service appointments may be necessary. See *If Unit Needs Service* (pg. 83).

Shaded box indicates service to be performed.

4 mos. or 4,000 miles	6 mos. or 6,000 miles	9 mos. or 9,000 miles	12 mos. or 12,000 miles

For scheduled maintenance beyond the first year, consult your authorized service provider.

Cleaning and Maintenance

Checking for Overheating

A key indicator that your Baby is operating properly is the unit's internal temperature. If Baby is running hot or cold, it may require service.

Temperature should be checked utilizing a certified gauge (sold separately). Follow manufacturer's instructions and insert only where directed. Your Baby is designed to give accurate temperature readings at the rear exhaust, the audio sensors, and under the extenders.

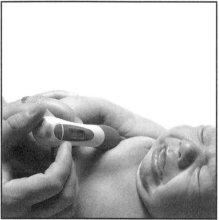

Checking temperature under extender. fig. 74a

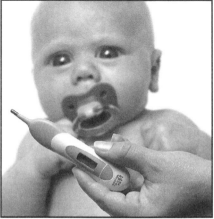

Use care and petroleum jelly when checking temperature at the rear exhaust. fig. 74b

Analyzing Temperature Check
Normal operating temperature range is between 96.8° and 99.5°F (36° and 37.5°C).

Call an authorized service provider immediately if operating temperature is:

• Below 95°F (35°C)
• 100.4°F (38°C) or higher and unit is 2 months or younger
• Above 100.4°F (38°C) for more than 24 hours with units of any age
• Above 101°F (38.3°C) after attempts to cool engine
• Above normal operating range and unit sounds continual audio alert

To cool engine:
• Add coolant fluids
• For units over 3 months, utilize aspirin-free additive
• Sponge unit with lukewarm water; air dry; repeat for one-half hour

Additional Info

Additional Info

Troubleshooting

Using the Troubleshooting Chart

Troubleshooting with your Baby will generally fall into one of the following categories:

Odors Baby is emitting unidentifiable smells.

Finish/Appearence Blemishes or irregularities on Baby's surface.

Filling Problems encountered during filling/refilling of Baby.

Sounds Baby is emitting noises.

Discharges Fluids and/or solids being ejected from Baby.

If your unit displays error messages during operation, use the Troubleshooting Chart to find the topic that best describes your situation. Follow the related solutions or preventive measures until you find one that helps. The Troubleshooting Chart is not intended to be a substitute for authorized service providers.

Troubleshooting (cont.)

Problem	Possible Cause	Solution	Preventive Measures
Baby emits strong odor	Gas	Allow time for odor to dissipate. You may also try placing scented candles around room. Be careful not to light match near source. See warning on pg. VI.	Avoid air bubbles when refilling to help reduce gas in Baby.
	Leakage	Carefully remove rear cover. Thoroughly clean exhaust area if needed.	None. Leakage is a normal occurrence and indicates your unit is running correctly.
Baby emits sour odor	Overspill during refilling	Check all crevices for spoiled liquid. Clean thoroughly.	Completely wipe down unit after each refilling.
Baby's processor is cone-shaped	Delivery of unit through small opening	Over time, unit's processor will lose cone shape.	Cesarean delivery.
Discoloration/ corrosion under rear cover	Trapped discharge or moisture combined with poor air circulation	Clean area and allow to air dry. Loosen or remove rear cover when possible.	Keep area clean and avoid use of cleaning agents. Change rear cover often. Use ointment to protect unit's surface from moisture.
Excessive swelling in undercarriage of unit	Unit is delivered with excess protective fluid encased in undercarriage	Over time, unit's undercarriage will resume normal size. Make note to service provider at next checkup.	None. Excessive swelling can be a normal occurrence.
Baby's thrusters are bowed	Packaging and storage in compact area prior to delivery	Over time, unit's thrusters should straighten out on their own. Make note to service provider at next checkup.	No known preventive measures.

WARNING: Do not place unit on or near electrical appliance while rear cover is removed. Risk of shock if leakage should occur.

77

Additional Info

Troubleshooting (cont.)

Problem	Possible Cause	Solution	Preventive Measures
Surface is blemished/ top of Baby is flaking	Unit's finish is adjusting to local environment	Most surface blemishes will diminish with time. Flaking may be treated by applying a lubricant.	Generally, unit's finish should be kept clean and dry. Some imperfections are common and add to the individuality of your unit.
Baby struggles to breathe while filling from breast station	Breasts are too large and may be blocking unit's intake valves	Pull breast away from air intake valves with fingers.	Keep air intake valves unobstructed.
Baby won't refill	Unit is full	Let unit rest 30–60 minutes and try to refill again.	Increase time between refillings. Unit will generally sound alarm if too much time has passed.
	Gas	Release excess gas. Try to refill again.	Gas is normal for new units. Proper refilling may help alleviate problem.
	Unit is tired	Allow unit to rest. Try to refill again.	Maintain a consistent schedule to ensure unit gets proper rest.
Baby continuously needs fuel	Growth spurt	Continue refilling on demand.	None. Unit self-regulates fuel intake.
Baby emits a loud, continuous, high-pitched sound	Empty fuel tank	Refill unit.	Keep unit on a regular filling and storing schedule to help reduce occurrence of loud noises. Avoid planes, restaurants and churches when possible.
	Leakage	Check rear cover. Change if necessary.	
	Unit is overtired	Store unit.	
	Gas	Release excess air. In severe cases anti-gas solution may be utilized.	

CAUTION: If problem is not resolved in a timely manner, unit may overheat.

Troubleshooting (cont.)

Problem	Possible Cause	Solution	Preventive Measures
Distorted sound/ unidentifiable language	Undeveloped language	None. Gurgles, squeals, shrieks, etc. are normal with your unit and indicate a healthy and active Baby.	None. With ongoing interaction and encouragement, unit's language will advance to actual words. Warning: Do not encourage such advanced operation until you are fully prepared to relinquish silence entirely.
Disruptive explosions inside rear cover	Gas being expelled from immature system	Over time, unit's system will develop and become less disruptive.	Problem is normal, especially for units that are refilled using breast stations. Symptoms may be reduced by refilling with artificial fuel using bottle.
Baby is ejecting fuel from intake valve	Fuel not properly absorbed, or unit has been overfilled	Clean unit; comfort if necessary. Unit may be full. If problem persists, contact an authorized service provider.	Do not top off while refilling. Avoid tossing or spinning unit within 30 minutes of refilling.
Clear liquid leaking from intake valve	Unit's teeth are developing	Apply a numbing gel to gums and/or insert chilled teething ring in intake valve. While this may temporarily soothe unit, leaking may continue.	Keep bib on unit and wipe cloth handy.
Tarry, green/black substance leaking under rear cover	Post-delivery release of packaging material	Within a day or two, unit will halt production of this discharge. If problem persists, contact an authorized service provider.	None. This is a normal occurrence and indicates your Baby's self-cleaning system is functioning properly.
Constant discharge from rear exhaust	Unit is properly digesting	Keep area clean. Continue to refill.	Check and change rear cover as often as necessary.

79

Additional Info

Frequently Asked Questions

Q. My Baby's processor is huge and his discharge hose is small. Is this normal?

A. Some of your Baby's parts may seem disproportionately large or small upon delivery. Size at time of delivery is no indication of a Baby's intelligence or functionality.

Q. My Baby has dark fuzz on its surface, particularly on its back. Can I shave it?

A. Do not remove surface fuzz on unit. It will disappear on its own within a few weeks.

Q. My unit is shrinking! She's lost nearly half a pound already.

A. The weight of most new units will decrease by 5 to 10% in the first 100 hours of operation. This is due to loss of internal fluids and packing materials. If your unit's weight does not increase, or if it continues to decrease, contact your authorized service provider.

Q. My Baby is turning yellow. Is he getting ripe?

A. A yellow tint to a new unit's finish is an indication of jaundice. The yellowing comes from the unit producing more bilirubin in the blood than the unit's liver can remove. Although it is common, you should take your unit in for service by an authorized provider.

Q. My unit seems to be smaller than others. Should I be concerned?

A. Remember that each Baby is individually crafted, so size specifications will vary. If your unit was delivered ahead of schedule, it's likely that its size will grow to more closely match other units over the coming months and years.

Q. My unit's exhaust is extremely loud. Do they make mufflers for Babies?

A. Many new units backfire loudly while discharging. This is normal and should subside within the first 1,500 hours of operation, as the Baby breaks in its fuel lines. Baby mufflers are not an after-market option.

Q. My unit is really ugly. Can I trade it in?

A. Because parts can shift during shipping, many new units are not at all attractive upon delivery. In time the unit's true features will become apparent. If at that time you still feel the same way about your unit, remember that in most cases a Baby is a combination of features taken from both you and your spouse. Refer to the Warranty on pg. 86.

Frequently Asked Questions (cont.)

Q. My Baby's audio alert won't stop sounding. How can I disconnect it?
A. You cannot disconnect the Baby's audio alert system. Approximately one in five units are delivered with the colic function, causing the audio alert to sound continually, particularly between 5 and 8 P.M. Though it may seem as though the unit is malfunctioning, this behavior is within operating norms. Do not attempt to return your unit to the manufacturer or to otherwise exchange it.

Q. My husband is becoming jealous that our Baby monopolizes the breast station and that he isn't the one refilling unit. What can I do?
A. You may want to invest in a breast pump, a tool used to express fuel from the breast station for use in remote filling at a later time. Your husband can assist with the breast pump and then can refill your unit at the bottle terminal.

Q. My Baby's grippers are often attached to his discharge hose. Should I disconnect them?
A. No. Your Baby is utilizing new motor skills and exercising his inherent inquisitive nature.

Q. The rear exhaust on my Baby seems to be blocked. Do I need to take her in for service, or should I just use a plunger?
A. Rear blockage is not an uncommon occurrence and can usually be fixed at home after consulting with a service professional over the phone. Your service provider may have you move the Baby's thrusters in a bicycle motion, add small amounts of bran to Baby's solid fuels or give apple juice via a bottle terminal. If the problem continues, report it again to your service provider.

Q. I thought my unit was self-cleaning. Can this feature be added?
A. Self-cleaning is not an option that can be delivered on a new Baby. The frequency of cleanings will be somewhat reduced as your unit ages, but your unit won't learn to clean itself for many years.

Q. Do we need to provide a noise-free environment for our Baby to be in sleep mode?
A. No. In fact, some Babies require noise to sleep, which leads owners to vacuum two to three times daily.

Additional Info

Performance Chart

Functionality varies with each Baby. Use this chart only as a guide.

TIME SINCE DELIVERY	FUNCTIONS UNIT MAY MASTER	FUNCTIONS UNIT MAY BE LEARNING
1 month	• Lift processor slightly • Focus on your face • Eject fuel or discharge in your eye	• Respond to sound • Follow object moving 6″ in front of lenses
2 months	• Display panel mirrors your smile • Expanded audio, including coos and gurgles	• Hold processor steady when upright • Give you a head butt • Self-soothe by inserting gripper into intake valve
3 months	• Recognition of owner(s) • 8-hour sleep mode • Change sleep schedule without warning	• New audio includes laughter • Modified push-up • Can spot you sneaking away from crib on all fours
4 months	• Modified push-up • Hold processor steady • Use audio alarm to get what it wants	• Grasp items • Pull hair from owner's head
5 months	• Play with grippers and thrusters • Play with discharge hose (model XY-B only) • Roll over (one way) • Get stuck in roll function	• Turn toward new sounds • Audio sensor recognizes personalized code name • Insert thrusters into intake valve • Insert nearly anything into intake valve
6 months	• Turn toward new sounds • Roll in both directions • Won't stay still for rear cover attachment	• Reach for objects • Sit without support • Ready for solid fuel • Produce toxic-smelling exhaust
7 months	• Reach for objects • Sit without support • Fall off couch	• Enhanced mobility via crawl • Combine syllables into word-like sounds
8 months	• Say "dada" and "mama" • Refer to "dada" as "mama"	• Point at desired object • Desire everything
9 months	• Make word-like sounds • Stand while holding on to things • Fall while holding on to things	• Pick up objects • Continually throw them to the floor
10 months	• Crawl well • Continually end up at neighbor's	• Recognize "no" command • Ignore "no" command
11 months	• Play Pat-a-Cake • Stand alone for a few seconds	• Put objects into containers • Hide your keys
12 months	• Jabber word-like sounds • Jabber relentlessly	• Take a few steps without help • Continually want to take steps with help

If Unit Needs Service

If you experience problems with your Baby that cannot be solved by referencing the *Troubleshooting* or *Frequently Asked Questions* sections of this manual, your unit may need professional service and/or repair. Consult your telephone or insurance directory under "Physicians — Pediatrics" for the nearest authorized service provider.

Especially during the first 3 months of operation, call your authorized service provider immediately* if unit:

• Overheats (see *Checking for Overheating,* pg. 74)

• Is abnormally quiet

• Emits loud noises more than usual, or of different type over a 1-hour period

• Refuses two successive fillings or does not indicate low fuel for 8 hours

• Seems particularly irritable or restless

Call for emergency service* if unit:

• Emits green discharge from intake valve

• Has an operating temperature over 102.2°F (39°C) for more than half an hour

• Discharges from intake valve AND emits loud noises uncontrollably

• Emits noise as if in pain and exterior color turns pale

• Discharges abnormal substances from rear exhaust

*When asking for help or service: Please provide a detailed description of the problem, your unit's complete model number, and date of acquisition. This information will help your service provider respond properly to your request.

Additional Info

Product Specifications

Fill in the information indicated and retain for future reference.

Owner Name(s): _____

Model No.: _____

Delivery Date: _____

Delivery Site: _____

Personalized Code Name: _____

Product Registration No.: _____

Exterior Color: _____

Lens Color at Delivery: _____

Options (check where applicable):
   ❑ Processor cover
      Color: _____
   ❑ Convex Cord Socket
   ❑ Converted Nozzle

Additional Info

Product Specifications (cont.)

ENGLISH

	Height	Weight	Processor Circumference
At Delivery:			
1 month:			
2 months:			
3 months:			
4 months:			
5 months:			
6 months:			
7 months:			
8 months:			
9 months:			
10 months:			
11 months:			
12 months:			

BABY

Our Satisfaction Promise*

**BABY-XX-G
BABY-XY-B**

To the Owner, we guarantee you will be 100% satisfied with your new Baby. If you are not satisfied and you wish to return the unit, be assured it is only a temporary condition brought on by sleep deprivation. Product returns are not accepted and will be shipped back at owner's expense. It's too late to turn back now. You'll thank us later.

*This promise does not extend to any accessories or additional items that did not accompany your unit upon delivery.

SAVE THESE INSTRUCTIONS FOR
FUTURE REFERENCE